GOD STILL SPEAKS

by

A. W. TOZER

pastor, preacher, author, magazine editor, spiritual mentor

2014
CROSSREACH PUBLICATIONS
KERRY, IRELAND

This edition © 2014 CrossReach Publications, Kerry, Ireland

Hope. Inspiration. Trust.

WE'RE SOCIAL! FOLLOW US FOR NEW TITLES AND DEALS:
FACEBOOK.COM/CROSSREACHPUBLICATIONS
TWITTER HANDLE: @CROSSREACHPUB

AVAILABLE IN PAPERBACK AND EBOOK EDITIONS
PLEASE GO ONLINE FOR MORE GREAT TITLES
AVAILABLE THROUGH CROSSREACH PUBLICATIONS.
AND IF YOU ENJOYED THIS BOOK PLEASE CONSIDER LEAVING A
REVIEW ON AMAZON. THAT HELPS US OUT A LOT. THANKS.

THE TEXT OF THIS BOOK IS IN THE PUBLIC DOMAIN. ALL OTHER
RIGHTS ARE RESERVED, INCLUDING THE RIGHT TO REPRODUCE
THIS EDITION OR PORTIONS OF IT IN ANY FORM WHATSOEVER
WITHOUT PRIOR WRITTEN CONSENT FROM THE PUBLISHER.

CONTENTS

Introduction 5

REVELATION IS NOT ENOUGH.............................7

THE SPEAKING VOICE 21

THE MENACE OF THE RELIGIOUS MOVIE...........31

About CrossReach Publications 55

Bestselling Titles from CrossReach 57

INTRODUCTION

Tozer is as popular today as when he was living on the earth. He is respected right across the spectrum of Christianity, in circles that would disagree sharply with him doctrinally. Why is this? A. W. Tozer was a man who knew the voice of God. He shared this experience with every true child of God. With all those who are called by the grace of God to share in the mystical union that is possible with Him through His Son Jesus.

Tozer fought against much dryness and formality in his day. Considered a mighty man of God by most Evangelicals today, he was unconventional in his approach to spirituality and had no qualms about consulting everyone from Catholic Saints to German Protestant mystics for inspiration on how to experience God more fully.

Tozer, just like his Master, doesn't fit neatly into our theological boxes. He was a man after God's own heart and was willing to break the rules (man-made ones that is) to get there.

Here are two writings by Tozer that touch on the heart of this goal. *Revelation is Not Enough* and *The Speaking Voice*. A bonus chapter *The Menace of the Religious Movie* is included.

This is meat to sink your spiritual teeth into. Tozer's writings will show you the way to satisfy your spiritual hunger.—Dave Kinsella

Revelation Is Not Enough[1]

The key, the crux of this whole issue, is in verse 17. If any man *is willing to do God's will, he shall know.*

"About the midst of the feast Jesus went up into the temple, and taught. And the Jews marvelled, saying, How knoweth this man letters, having never learned? Jesus answered them, and said, My doctrine is not mine, but his that sent me. If any man will do his will, he shall know of the doctrine, whether it be of God, or whether I speak of myself" (John 7:14-17).

People marvelled at our Lord as He taught. They asked: "How knoweth this man letters having never learned?" 'How does He know learning', in other words, 'never having studied in the regular schools?' In those days they had no schools as we know them; a rabbi taught little groups of students. Our Lord evidently never attended a rabbinical school so they

---

[1] The following message by the late Dr. A. W. Tozer, to be included in a further volume of addresses by him now in preparation, is, we feel, so much in keeping with the ministry of A Witness and A Testimony, that we borrow it for our readers, assured that they will be very glad to read it. It was recently in The Alliance Witness of the Christian and Missionary Alliance. And while mentioning this, may I say that, in early years of ministry and the Lord's work, I owed very much to the life of Dr. A. B. Simpson, founder of that 'Alliance'.— T Austin-Sparks

asked: 'How does He get His wonderful doctrine, since He has never been to the schools of the rabbis?'

Now, this question tells us a good deal about these people. It tells us that they held truth to be intellectual merely, capable of being reduced to a code. To know truth it was necessary only to learn the code.

Most of them had no books of their own—they learned by memorizing. That was their conception of truth. I gather this not only from verse 17 but from the whole Gospel of John. To these people truth was an intellectual thing—just as we know that two times two is four.

That is truth, but it is an intellectual truth only. They reduced divine truth to that status. They knew the laws: "Thou shalt have no other gods before me.... Remember the sabbath day, to keep it holy.... Thou shalt not ...". But to them there was no mysterious depth in truth, nothing beneath and nothing beyond the obvious fact. It was exactly here that they parted company with our Saviour, for our Lord Jesus constantly taught the beyond and the beneath.

These people believed that the words of truth were the truth. And here is a basic misunderstanding of Christian theology with a moral and spiritual consequence that is vastly important. They believed that if you had the words of truth, if you could repeat the code of truth, you had the truth. That if you lived by the word of truth you lived in the truth.

The Saviour tried to correct this inadequate view. He showed them the heavenly quality of His message. He said: 'My doctrine is not Mine I am not a rabbi teaching doctrine that you can memorize and repeat. What I am giving you is not that kind of doctrine at all.'

He had said previously: 'I say nothing for Myself—what I see the Father do, that I do, and what the Father speaks, that I speak. What I have seen yonder I tell you about. I am a transparent medium through which the truth is being spoken. You believe that the way to truth is to go to a rabbi and learn it. That's not the truth, that approach to truth is inadequate.'

Here, it seems to me, is the weakness in modern Christianity. The battle line, the warfare today, is not necessarily between the fundamentalist and the liberal. There is a difference between them, of course. The fundamentalist says God made the heaven and the earth. The liberal says: 'Well, that's a poetic way of stating it; actually it came up by evolution.' The fundamentalist says Jesus Christ was the very Son of God. The liberal says: 'Well, He certainly was a wonderful man and He is the Master, but I don't quite know about His deity.' So there is a division, but I don't think the warfare is on these matters any more.

The battle has shifted to another more important field. The warfare, the dividing line today, is between evangelical rationalists and evangelical mystics. I will explain what I mean.

There is today an evangelical rationalism which is the same as these Jews had. They said the truth is in the word, and if you want to know truth, go to the rabbi and learn the word. If you get the word, you have got the truth. That is evangelical rationalism and we have that today in fundamental circles. 'If you learn the text you've got the truth.'

This evangelical rationalism will kill the truth just as quickly as liberalism will, though in more subtle way. The liberal stands over there and says: 'I don't believe your inspired Bible; I don't believe your deified Christ. I believe the Bibles in a way; it is the record of the high points of great men and I believe in a certain mystic communion with the universe and it is all very wonderful, but I don't believe as you do.'

You can easily spot this man—train your glasses on him and there he stands. You can tell he is on the other side, for he wears the uniform of the other side.

God Still Speaks

But your evangelical rationalist wears our uniform. He comes in wearing our uniform and says what the Pharisees, the worst enemies Jesus had while He was on earth, said: 'Well, truth is truth, and if you believe the truth you've got it.'

Such see no beyond and no mystic depth, no mysterious heights, nothing supernatural or divine. They see only: "I believe in God the Father Almighty, Maker of heaven and earth: and in Jesus Christ His only Son, our Lord." They have the text and the code and the creed, and to them that is the truth. So they pass it on to others. The result is we are dying spiritually.

Now, what about the evangelical mystic? I don't really like the word 'mystic' because you think of a fellow with long hair and a little goatee who acts dreamy and strange. Maybe it is not a good word at all, but I am talking about the spiritual side of things—that the truth is more than the text. There is something that you've got to get through to. The truth is more than the code. There is a heart beating in the middle of the code and you've got to get there.

Now the question is simply this: Is the body of Christian truth enough? Or does truth have a soul as well as a body? The evangelical rationalist says that all of that talk about the soul of truth is poetic nonsense. The body of truth is all you need; if you believe the body of truth you are on your way to heaven and you can't backslide and everything will be alright and you will get a crown in the last day.

Now otherwise stated: Is revelation enough or must there be illumination? Is this Bible an inspired book? Is it a revealed book? Of course you and I believe that it is a revelation, that God spoke all these words and holy men spoke as they were moved by the Holy Ghost.

I believe that this Bible is a living book, that God has given it to us and that we dare not add to it or take away from it. It is revelation. But revelation is not enough. There must be illumination before revelation can get to your soul. It isn't enough that I hold an inspired book in my hands. I must have an inspired heart. There is the difference.

You can memorize all the texts of the Bible—and I believe in memorizing—but when you are through you've got nothing but the body. There is the soul of truth as well as the body. There is a divine inward illumination the Holy Ghost must give us or we don't know what truth means.

Conversion is a miraculous act of God by the Holy Ghost; it must be wrought in the spirit. The body of truth is not enough; there must be an inward illumination.

God Still Speaks

Christ's conflict was with the theological rationalist. It revealed itself in the Sermon on the Mount and the whole Book of John. Just as Colossians argues against Manichaeism and Galatians argues against Jewish legalism, so the Book of John is a long, inspired, passionately outpoured book trying to save us from evangelical rationalism, the doctrine that says the text is enough. Textualism is as deadly as liberalism.

Now revelation, I repeat, can't save. Revelation is the ground upon which we stand. Revelation tells us what to believe. It is the Book of God and I stand for it with all my heart; but there must be, before I can be saved, illumination, penitence, renewal, inward deliverance.

I have no doubt that many people are eased into the kingdom. They are jockeyed into believing in the text, and they do; but they have never been illuminated by the Holy Ghost. They have never been renewed in their hearts. They never get into the kingdom at all.

Now, there is a secret in divine truth altogether hidden from the unprepared soul. This is where we stand in the terrible day in which we live. Christianity is not something you just reach up and grab. There must be a preparation of the mind, a preparation of the life and a preparation of the inner man before we can savingly believe in Jesus Christ.

Somebody asks: Is it possible to hear the truth and not understand the truth? Listen to Isaiah: "Hear ye indeed, but understand not, and see ye indeed, but perceive not" (6:9). It is possible to see yet not perceive.

Paul says (1 Corinthians 2:4-5): "My speech and my preaching was not with enticing words of man's wisdom, but in demonstration of the Spirit and of power: that your faith should not stand in the wisdom of men, but in the power of God."

Now the theological rationalists say that your faith should stand not in the wisdom of man but in the Word of God. Paul didn't say that at all. He said your faith should stand in the *power of God*. That's quite a different thing.

Verses 9 through 14 say: "Eye hath not seen, nor ear heard, neither have entered into the heart of man, the things which God hath prepared for them that love him. But God hath revealed them unto us by his Spirit: for the Spirit searcheth all things, yea, the deep things of God. For what man knoweth the things of man, save the spirit of man which is in him? even so the things of God knoweth no man, but the Spirit of God.... But the natural man receiveth not the things of the Spirit of God: for they are foolishness unto him: neither can he know them, because they are spiritually discerned."

God Still Speaks

Paul, the man of God, is saying: I came preaching and I preached with power that would illuminate and get to the conscience and to the spirit and change the inner man in order that your faith might stand in the power of God.

My brethren, your faith can stand in the text and you can be as dead as the proverbial doornail, but when the power of God moves in on the text and sets the sacrifice on fire, then you have Christianity. We call that revival, but it's not revival at all. It is simply New Testament Christianity. It's what it ought to have been in the first place, but was not.

Now look at Matthew 11: "Jesus answered and said, I thank thee O Father, Lord of heaven and earth, because thou hast hid these things from the wise and prudent, and hast revealed them unto babes. Even so, Father: for so it seemed good in thy sight. All things are delivered unto me of my Father: and no man knoweth the Son, but the Father, neither knoweth any man the Father, save the Son, and he to whomsoever the Son will reveal him."

So there we have the doctrine taught plainly that there is not only a body of truth which we must hold at our peril; there is also a soul in that body which we must get through to, and if we don't get through to the soul of truth we have only a dead body on our hands.

A. W. Tozer

A church can go on holding the creed. and the truth for years and generations and grow old and die, and new people come up and receive that same code and they grow old and die.

Then some revivalist comes in and gets everybody stirred and prayer moves God down on the scene and revival comes to that church. People who thought they were saved get saved. People who have only believed in a code now believe in Christ.

A man will go along in a church and believe texts and quote them and memorize them and teach them and maybe become a deacon and all the rest. Then one day, under the fiery preaching of some visitor or maybe the pastor, he suddenly feels himself terribly in need of God and he forgets all his past history and goes to his knees and like David begins to pour out his soul in confession. Then he leaps to his feet and testifies: 'I've been a deacon in this church twenty-six years and never was born again until tonight.'

What happened? That man had been trusting the dead body of truth until some inspired preacher let him know that truth has a soul. Or maybe God taught him in secret that truth had a soul as well as a body and he dared to get through and pursue by penitence and obedience until God honoured his faith and flashed the light on. And like lightning out of heaven it touched his spirit and all the texts he had memorized became alive.

God Still Speaks

Thank God, he did memorize the texts and all the truth he knew suddenly now bloomed in the light. That is why I believe we ought to memorize. That is why we ought to get to know the Word, why we ought to fill our minds with the songs and the great hymns of the church. They won't mean anything to us until the Holy Ghost comes. But when He comes He will have fuel to use. Fire without fuel won't burn but fuel without fire is dead. And the Holy Ghost will not come on a church where there is no Biblical fuel. There must be Bible teaching. We must have the body of truth.

Jesus said if any man is willing to do God's will, he shall *know*—he shall know the doctrine, he shall know the teaching. Now, this body of truth can be grasped by the average, normal intellect. You can grasp truth, but only the enlightened soul will ever know the truth and only the prepared heart will ever be enlightened.

And just what is the preparation needed? Jesus said: 'If any man *is willing to do My will* the light will flash in on him. If any man will obey Me, God will enlighten his soul immediately.'

We make Jesus Christ a convenience. We make Him a lifeboat to get us to shore, a guide to find us when we are lost. We reduce Him simply to Big Friend to help us when we are in trouble.

That is not Christianity. Jesus Christ is Lord. But when a man is willing to do His will, he is repenting and the truth flashes in.

No man can know the Son except the Father tell him. No man can know the Father except the Son reveal Him. I can know about God, that's the body of truth. But I can't know God, the soul of truth, unless I am ready to be obedient.

Before the Word of God can mean anything inside of me there must be obedience to the Word. Truth will not give itself to a rebel. Truth will not impart life to a man who will not obey the light! "If we walk in the light, as he is in the light, we have fellowship one with another, and the blood of Jesus Christ his Son cleanseth us from all sin." If you are disobeying Jesus Christ you can't expect to be enlightened.

But there is illumination. I know what Charles Wesley meant when he wrote: "His spirit answers to the blood, And tells me I am born of God!" Nobody had to come and tell me what he meant. 'He that is willing to do My will,' said Jesus, 'shall have a revelation to his own heart. He shall have an inward illumination that tells him he is a child of God.'

If a sinner goes to the altar and a worker with a marked New Testament argues him into the kingdom, the devil will meet him two blocks down the street and argue him out of it again. But if he has an inward illumination and he has that witness within because the Spirit answers to the blood, you can't argue with that man. He will say: 'But I *know*.' A man like that is not bigoted or arrogant, he is just sure.

Now that's revival, but yet it is not revival either; it is normal Christianity. It's the way we should be. "If any man will do his will, he shall know."

But you say you're going to take a Bible course. If you are holding out on God, refusing to follow Jesus, you can take a course and learn all about synthesis and analysis and all the rest. But you might just as well read Pogo; all the courses in the world won't illuminate you inside. You can fill your head full of knowledge, but the day that you decide you are going to obey God it will get down into your heart. You shall know. Only the servants of truth can ever know truth. Only those who obey can ever have the inward change.

You can stand on the outside and can know all about it. I once read a book about the inner spiritual life by a man who was not a Christian at all. He had an amazing penetration. He was a sharp intellectual, a keen Englishman. He stood outside and examined spiritual people from the outside but nothing ever reached him.

A. W. Tozer

You can read your Bible—read any version you want—and if you are honest you will admit that it is either obedience or inward blindness. You can repeat the Book of Romans word for word and still be blind inwardly. You can quote the whole Book of Psalms and still be blind inwardly. You can know the doctrine of justification by faith and take your stand with Luther and the Reformation, and be blind inwardly. For it is not the body of truth that enlightens; it is the Spirit of truth that enlightens.

If you are willing to obey the Lord Jesus He will illuminate your spirit, inwardly enlighten you, and the truth you have known will now be known spiritually and power will begin to flow up and out and you will find yourself changed, marvellously changed. In that great day of Christ's coming all that will matter is whether or not I have been inwardly illuminated. Inwardly regenerated. Inwardly purified.

Do I *know* Jesus?

The Speaking Voice

In the beginning was the Word, and the Word was with God, and the Word was God.—John 1:1

An intelligent plain man, untaught in the truths of Christianity, coming upon this text, would likely conclude that John meant to teach that it is the nature of God to speak, to communicate His thoughts to others. And he would be right. A word is a medium by which thoughts are expressed, and the application of the term to the Eternal Son leads us to believe that self-expression is inherent in the Godhead, that God is forever seeking to speak Himself out to His creation. The whole Bible supports the idea. God is speaking. Not God spoke, but God is speaking. He is by His nature continuously articulate. He fills the world with His speaking Voice.

One of the great realities with which we have to deal is the Voice of God in His world. The briefest and only satisfying cosmogony is this: "He spake and it was done." The why of natural law is the living Voice of God immanent in His creation. And this word of God which brought all worlds into being cannot be understood to mean the Bible, for it is not a written or printed word at all, but the expression of the will of God spoken into the structure of all things. This word of God is the breath of God filling the world with living potentiality. The Voice of God is the most powerful force in nature, indeed the only force in nature, for all energy is here only because the power-filled Word is being spoken.

The Bible is the written word of God, and because it is written it is confined and limited by the necessities of ink and paper and leather. The Voice of God, however, is alive and free as the sovereign God is free. "The words that I speak unto you, they are spirit, and they are life." The life is in the speaking words. God's word in the Bible can have power only because it corresponds to God's word in the universe. It is the present Voice which makes the written Word all-powerful. Otherwise it would lie locked in slumber within the covers of a book.

We take a low and primitive view of things when we conceive of God at the creation coming into physical contact with things, shaping and fitting and building like a carpenter. The Bible teaches otherwise: "By the word of the Lord were the heavens made; and all the host of them by the breath of his mouth. . . . For he spake, and it was done; he commanded, and it stood fast." "Through faith we understand that the worlds were framed by the word of God." Again we must remember that God is referring here not to His written Word, but to His speaking Voice. His world-filling Voice is meant, that Voice which antedates the Bible by uncounted centuries, that Voice which has not been silent since the dawn of creation, but is sounding still throughout the full far reaches of the universe.

The Word of God is quick and powerful. In the beginning He spoke to nothing, and it became something. Chaos heard it and became order; darkness heard it and became light. "And God said—and it was so." These twin phrases, as cause and effect, occur throughout the Genesis story of the creation. The said accounts for the so. The so is the said put into the Continuous present.

That God is here and that He is speaking—these truths are back of all other Bible truths; without them there could be no revelation at all. God did not write a book and send it by messenger to be read at a distance by unaided minds. He spoke a Book and lives in His spoken words, constantly speaking His words and causing the power of them to persist across the years. God breathed on clay and it became a man; He breathes on men and they become clay. "Return ye children of men," was the word spoken at the Fall by which God decreed the death of every man, and no added word has He needed to speak. The sad procession of mankind across the face of the earth from birth to the grave is proof that His original Word was enough.

We have not given sufficient attention to that deep utterance in the Book of John, "That was the true Light, which lighteth every man that cometh into the world." Shift the punctuation around as we will and the truth is still there: the Word of God affects the hearts of all men as light in the soul. In the hearts of all men the light shines, the Word sounds, and there is no escaping them. Something like this would of necessity be so if God is alive and in His world. And John says that it is so. Even those persons who have never heard of the Bible have still been preached to with sufficient clarity to remove every excuse from their hearts forever. "Which show the work of the law written in their hearts, their conscience also bearing Witness, and their thoughts the mean while either accusing or else excusing one another." "For the invisible things of him from the creation of the world are clearly seen, being understood by the things that are made, even his eternal power and Godhead; so that they are without excuse."

This universal Voice of God was by the ancient Hebrews often called Wisdom, and was said to be everywhere sounding and searching throughout the earth, seeking some response from the Sons of men. The eighth chapter of the Book of Proverbs begins, "Doth not wisdom cry? and understanding put forth her voice?" The writer then pictures wisdom as a beautiful woman standing "in the top of the high places, by the way in the places of the paths." She sounds her voice from every quarter so that no one may miss hearing it. "Unto you, O men, I call; and my voice is to the sons of men." Then she pleads for the simple and the foolish to give ear to her words.

God Still Speaks

It is spiritual response for which this Wisdom of God is pleading, a response which she has always sought and is but rarely able to secure. The tragedy is that our eternal welfare depends upon our hearing, and we have trained our ears not to hear.

This universal Voice has ever sounded, and it has often troubled men even when they did not understand the source of their fears. Could it be that this Voice distilling like a living mist upon the hearts of men has been the undiscovered cause of the troubled conscience and the longing for immortality confessed by millions since the dawn of recorded history? We need not fear to face up to this. The speaking Voice is a fact. How men have reacted to it is for any observer to note.

When God spoke out of heaven to our Lord, self-centered men who heard it explained it by natural causes: they said, "It thundered." This habit of explaining the Voice by appeals to natural law is at the very root of modern science. In the living breathing cosmos there is a mysterious Something, too wonderful, too awful for any mind to understand. The believing man does not claim to understand. He falls to his knees and whispers, "God." The man of earth kneels also, but not to worship. He kneels to examine, to search, to find the cause and the how of things. Just now we happen to be living in a secular age. Our thought habits are those of the scientist, not those of the worshipper.

We are more likely to explain than to adore. "It thundered," we exclaim, and go our earthly way. But still the Voice sounds and searches. The order and life of the world depend upon that Voice, but men are mostly too busy or too stubborn to give attention.

Every one of us has had experiences which we have not been able to explain: a sudden sense of loneliness, or a feeling of wonder or awe in the face of the universal vastness. Or we have had a fleeting visitation of light like an illumination from some other sun, giving us in a quick flash an assurance that we are from another world, that our origins are divine. What we saw there, or felt, or heard, may have been contrary to all that we had been taught in the schools and at wide variance with all our former beliefs and opinions. We were forced to suspend our acquired doubts while, for a moment, the clouds were rolled back and we saw and heard for ourselves. Explain such things as we will, I think we have not been fair to the facts until we allow at least the possibility that such experiences may arise from the Presence of God in the world and His persistent effort to communicate with mankind. Let us not dismiss such a hypothesis too flippantly.

It is my own belief (and here I shall not feel bad if no one follows me) that every good and beautiful thing which man has produced in the world has been the result of his faulty and sin-blocked response to the creative Voice sounding over the earth. The moral philosophers who dreamed their high dreams of virtue, the religious thinkers who speculated about God and immortality, the poets and artists who created out of common stuff pure and lasting beauty: how can we explain them? It is not enough to say simply, "It was genius." What then is genius? Could it be that a genius is a man haunted by the speaking Voice, laboring and striving like one possessed to achieve ends which he only vaguely understands? That the great man may have missed God in his labors, that he may even have spoken or written against God does not destroy the idea I am advancing. God's redemptive revelation in the Holy Scriptures is necessary to saving faith and peace with God. Faith in a risen Saviour is necessary if the vague stirrings toward immortality are to bring us to restful and satisfying communion with God. To me this is a plausible explanation of all that is best out of Christ. But you can be a good Christian and not accept my thesis.

The Voice of God is a friendly Voice. No one need fear to listen to it unless he has already made up his mind to resist it. The blood of Jesus has covered not only the human race but all creation as well. "And having made peace through the blood of his cross, by him to reconcile all things unto himself; by him, I say, whether they be things in earth, or things in heaven." We may safely preach a friendly Heaven. The heavens as well as the earth are filled with the good will of Him that dwelt in the bush. The perfect blood of atonement secures this forever.

Whoever will listen will hear the speaking Heaven. This is definitely not the hour when men take kindly to an exhortation to listen, for listening is not today a part of popular religion. We are at the opposite end of the pole from there. Religion has accepted the monstrous heresy that noise, size, activity and bluster make a man dear to God. But we may take heart. To a people caught in the tempest of the last great conflict God says, "Be still, and know that I am God," and still He says it, as if He means to tell us that our strength and safety lie not in noise but in silence.

It is important that we get still to wait on God. And it is best that we get alone, preferably with our Bible outspread before us. Then if we will we may draw near to God and begin to hear Him speak to us in our hearts. I think for the average person the progression will be something like this: First a sound as of a Presence walking in the garden. Then a voice, more intelligible, but still far from clear. Then the happy moment when the Spirit begins to illuminate the Scriptures, and that which had been only a sound, or at best a voice, now becomes an intelligible word, warm and intimate and clear as the word of a dear friend. Then will come life and light, and best of all, ability to see and rest in and embrace Jesus Christ as Saviour and Lord and All.

God Still Speaks

The Bible will never be a living Book to us until we are convinced that God is articulate in His universe. To jump from a dead, impersonal world to a dogmatic Bible is too much for most people. They may admit that they should accept the Bible as the Word of God, and they may try to think of it as such, but they find it impossible to believe that the words there on the page are actually for them. A man may say, "These words are addressed to me," and yet in his heart not feel and know that they are. He is the victim of a divided psychology. He tries to think of God as mute everywhere else and vocal only in a book.

I believe that much of our religious unbelief is due to a wrong conception of and a wrong feeling for the Scriptures of Truth. A silent God suddenly began to speak in a book and when the book was finished lapsed back into silence again forever. Now we read the book as the record of what God said when He was for a brief time in a speaking mood. With notions like that in our heads how can we believe? The facts are that God is not silent, has never been silent. It is the nature of God to speak. The second Person of the Holy Trinity is called the Word. The Bible is the inevitable outcome of God's continuous speech. It is the infallible declaration of His mind for us put into our familiar human words.

I think a new world will arise out of the religious mists when we approach our Bible with the idea that it is not only a book which was once spoken, but a book which is now speaking. The prophets habitually said, "Thus saith the Lord." They meant their hearers to understand that God's speaking is in the continuous present. We may use the past tense properly to indicate that at a certain time a certain word of God was spoken, but a word of God once spoken continues to be spoken, as a child once born continues to be alive, or a world once created continues to exist. And those are but imperfect illustrations, for children die and worlds burn out, but the Word of our God endureth forever.

If you would follow on to know the Lord, come at once to the open Bible expecting it to speak to you. Do not come with the notion that it is a thing which you may push around at your convenience. It is more than a thing; it is a voice, a word, the very Word of the living God.

The Menace of the Religious Movie

When God gave to Moses the blueprint of the Tabernacle He was careful to include every detail; then, lest Moses should get the notion that he could improve on the original plan, God warned him solemnly, "And look that thou make them after their pattern, which was shown thee in the mount." God, not Moses, was the architect. To decide the plan was the prerogative of the Deity. No one dare alter it so much as a hairbreadth.

The New Testament Church also is built after a pattern. Not the doctrines only but the methods are divinely given. The doctrines are expressly stated in so many words. Some of the methods followed by the early New Testament Church had been given by direct command; others were used by God's specific approval, having obviously been commanded the apostles by the Spirit. The point is that when the New Testament canon was closed the blueprint for the age was complete. God has added nothing since that time.

From God's revealed plan we depart at our peril. Every departure has two consequences, the immediate and the remote. The immediate touches the individual and those close to him; the remote extends into the future to unknown times, and may expand so far as to influence for evil the whole Church of God on earth.

The temptation to introduce "new" things into the work of God has always been too strong for some people to resist. The Church has suffered untold injury at the hands of well intentioned but misguided persons who have felt that they know more about running God's work than Christ and His apostles did. A solid train of box cars would not suffice to haul away the religious truck which has been brought into the service of the Church with the hope of improving on the original pattern. These things have been, one and all, positive hindrances to the progress of the Truth, and have so altered the divinely-planned structure that the apostles, were they to return to earth today, would scarcely recognize the misshapen thing which has resulted.

Our Lord while on earth cleansed the Temple, and periodic cleansings have been necessary in the Church of God throughout the centuries. Every generation is sure to have its ambitious amateur to come up with some shiny gadget which he proceeds to urge upon the priests before the altar. That the Scriptures do not justify its existence does not seem to bother him at all. It is brought in anyway and presented in the very name of Orthodoxy. Soon it is identified in the minds of the Christian public with all that is good and holy. Then, of course, to attack the gadget is to attack the Truth itself. This is an old familiar technique so often and so long practiced by the devotees of error that I marvel how the children of God can be taken in by it.

We of the evangelical faith are in the rather awkward position of criticizing Roman Catholicism for its weight of unscriptural impedimenta and at the same time tolerating in our own churches a world of religious fribble as bad as holy water or the elevated host. Heresy of method may be as deadly as heresy of message. Old-line Protestantism has long ago been smothered to death

God Still Speaks

by extra-scriptural rubbish. Unless we of the gospel churches wake up soon we shall most surely die by the same means.

Within the last few years a new method has been invented for imparting spiritual knowledge; or, to be more accurate, it is not new at all, but is an adaptation of a gadget of some years standing, one which by its origin and background belongs not to the Church but to the world. Some within the fold of the Church have thrown their mantle over it, have "blessed it with a text" and are now trying to show that it is the very gift of God for our day. But, however eloquent the sales talk, it is an unauthorized addition nevertheless, and was never a part of the pattern shown us on the mount.

I refer, of course, to the religious movie.

For the motion picture as such I have no irrational allergy. It is a mechanical invention merely and is in its essence amoral; that is, it is neither good nor bad, but neutral. With any physical object or any creature lacking the power of choice it could not be otherwise. Whether such an object is useful or harmful depends altogether upon who uses it and what he uses it for. No moral quality attaches where there is no free choice. Sin and righteousness lie in the will. The motion picture is in the same class as the automobile, the typewriter, or the radio: a powerful instrument for good or evil, depending upon how it is applied.

For teaching the facts of physical science the motion picture has been useful. The public schools have used it successfully to teach health habits to children. The army employed it to speed up instruction during the war. That it has been of real service within its limited field is freely acknowledged here.

Over against this is the fact that the motion picture in evil hands has been a source of moral corruption to millions. No one who values his reputation as a responsible adult will deny that the sex movie and the crime movie have done untold injury to the lives of countless young people in our generation. The harm lies not in the instrument itself, but in the evil will of those who use it for their own selfish ends.

I am convinced that the modern religious movie is an example of the harmful misuse of a neutral instrument. There are sound reasons for my belief. I am prepared to state them.

That I may be as clear as possible, let me explain what I do and do not mean by the religious movie. I do not mean the missionary picture nor the travel picture which aims to focus attention upon one or another section of the world's great harvest field. These do not come under consideration here.

By the religious movie I mean that type of motion picture which attempts to treat spiritual themes by dramatic representation. These are (as their advocates dare not deny) frank imitations of the authentic Hollywood variety, but the truth requires me to say that they are infinitely below their models, being mostly awkward, amateurish and, from an artistic standpoint, hopelessly and piteously bad.

These pictures are produced by acting a religious story before the camera. Take for example the famous and beautiful story of the Prodigal Son. This would be made

GOD STILL SPEAKS

into a movie by treating the narrative as a scenario. Stage scenery would be set up, actors would take the roles of Father, Prodigal Son, Elder Brother, etc. There would be plot, sequence and dramatic denouement as in the ordinary tear jerker shown at the Bijou movie house on Main Street in any one of a thousand American towns. The story would be acted out, photographed, run onto reels and shipped around the country to be shown for a few wherever desired.

The "service" where such a movie would be shown might seem much like any other service until time for the message from the Word of God. Then the lights would be put out and the picture turned on. The "message" would consist of this movie. What followed the picture would, of course, vary with the circumstances, but often an invitation song is sung and a tender appeal is made for erring sinners to return to God.

Now, what is wrong with all this? Why should any man object to this or go out of his way to oppose its use in the house of God? Here is my answer:

1. It violates the scriptural law of hearing.

The power of speech is a noble gift of God. In his ability to open his mouth and by means of words make his fellows know what is going on inside his mind, a man shares one of the prerogatives of the Creator. In its ability to understand the spoken word the human mind rises unique above all the lower creation. The gift which enables a man to translate abstract ideas into sounds is a badge of his honor as made in the image of God.

Written or printed words are sound symbols and are translated by the mind into hearing. Hieroglyphics and ideograms were, in effect, not pictures but letters, and the letters were agreed-upon marks which stood for agreed-upon ideas. Thus words, whether spoken or written, are a medium for the communication of ideas. This is basic in human nature and stems from our divine origin.

It is significant that when God gave to mankind His great redemptive revelation He couched it in words. "And God spake all these words" very well sums up the Bible's own account of how it got here. "Thus saith the Lord" is the constant refrain of the prophets. "The words that I speak unto you, they are spirit, and they are life," said our Lord to His hearers. Again He said, "He that heareth my word, and believeth on him that sent me, hath everlasting life." Paul made words and faith to be inseparable: "Faith cometh by hearing, and hearing by the word of God." And he also said, "How shall they hear without a preacher?" (Romans 10:14)

Surely it requires no genius to see that the Bible rules out pictures and dramatics as media for bringing faith and life to the human soul.

The plain fact is that no vital spiritual truth can be expressed by a picture. Actually all any picture can do is to recall to mind some truth already learned through the familiar medium of the spoken or written word. Religious instruction and words are bound together by a living cord and cannot be separated without fatal loss. The Spirit Himself, teaching soundlessly within the heart, makes use of ideas previously received into the mind by means of words.

If I am reminded that modern religious movies are "sound" pictures, making use of the human voice to

God Still Speaks

augment the dramatic action, the answer is easy. Just as far as the movie depends upon spoken words it makes pictures unnecessary; the picture is the very thing that differentiates between the movie and the sermon. The movie addresses its message primarily to the eye, and the ear only incidentally. Were the message addressed to the ear as in the Scriptures, the picture would have no meaning and could be omitted without loss to the intended effect. Words can say all that God intends them to say, and this they can do without the aid of pictures.

According to one popular theory the mind receives through the eye five times as much information as the ear. As far as the external shell of physical facts is concerned this may hold good, but when we come to spiritual truth we are in another world entirely. In that world the outer eye is not too important. God addresses His message to the hearing ear. "We look," says Paul, "not at the things which are seen, but at the things which are not seen: for the things which are seen are temporal; but the things which are not seen are eternal" (2 Corinthians 4:18). This agrees with the whole burden of the Bible, which teaches us that we should withdraw our eyes from beholding visible things, and fasten the eyes of our hearts upon God while we reverently listen to His uttered words.

"The word is nigh thee, even in thy mouth, and in thy heart: that is, the word of faith, which we preach" (Romans 10:8). Here, and not somewhere else, is the New Testament pattern, and no human being, and no angel from heaven has any right to alter that pattern.

2. The religious movie embodies the mischievous notion that religion is, or can be made, a form of entertainment.

A. W. Tozer

This notion has come upon us lately like a tidal wave and is either openly taught or tacitly assumed by increasing numbers of people. Since it is inextricably bound up with the subject under discussion I had better say more about it.

The idea that religion should be entertaining has made some radical changes in the evangelical picture within this generation. It has given us not only the "gospel" movie but a new type of religious journalism as well. It has created a new kind of magazine for church people, which can be read from cover to cover without effort, without thought—and without profit. It has also brought a veritable flood of religious fiction with plastic heroines and bloodless heroes like no one who has ever lived upon this well known terrestrial ball.

That religion and amusement are forever opposed to each other by their very essential natures is apparently not known to this new school of religious entertainers. Their effort to slip up on the reader and administer a quick shot of saving truth while his mind is on something else is not only futile, it is, in fact, not too far short of being plain dishonest. The hope that they can convert a man while he is occupied with the doings of some imaginary hero reminds one of the story of the Catholic missionary who used to sneak up on sick people and children and splash a little holy water on them to guarantee their passage to the city of gold.

I believe that most responsible religious teachers will agree that any effort to teach spiritual truth through entertainment is at best futile and at worst positively injurious to the soul. But entertainment pays off, and the economic consideration is always a powerful one in deciding what shall and what shall not be offered to the public—even in the churches.

Deep spiritual experiences come only from much study, earnest prayer and long meditation. It is true that men by thinking cannot find God; it is also true that men cannot know God very well without a lot of reverent thinking. Religious movies, by appealing directly to the shallowest stratum of our minds, cannot but create bad mental habits which unfit the soul for the reception of genuine spiritual impressions.

Religious movies are mistakenly thought by some people to be blessed of the Lord because many come away from them with moist eyes. If this is a proof of God's blessing, then we might as well go the whole way and assert that every show that brings tears is of God. Those who attend the theater know how often the audiences are moved to tears by the joys and sorrows of the highly paid entertainers who kiss and emote and murder and die for the purpose of exciting the spectators to a high pitch of emotional excitement. Men and women who are dedicated to sin and appointed to death may nevertheless weep in sympathy for the painted actors and be not one bit the better for it. The emotions have had a beautiful time, but the will is left untouched. The religious movie is sure to draw together a goodly number of persons who cannot distinguish the twinges of vicarious sympathy from the true operations of the Holy Ghost.

3. The religious movie is a menace to true religion because it embodies acting, a violation of sincerity.

Without doubt the most precious thing any man possesses is his individuated being; that by which he is himself and not someone else; that which cannot be finally voided by the man himself nor shared with another. Each one of us, however humble our place in the social scheme, is unique in creation. Each is a new whole man possessing his own separate "I-ness" which makes him forever something apart, an individual human being. It is this quality of uniqueness which permits a man to enjoy every reward of virtue and makes him responsible for every sin. It is his selfness, which will persist forever, and which distinguishes him from every creature which has been or ever will be created.

Because man is such a being as this all moral teachers, and especially Christ and His apostles, make sincerity to be basic in the good life. The word, as the New Testament uses it, refers to the practice of holding fine pottery up to the sun to test it for purity. In the white light of the sun all foreign substances were instantly exposed. So the test of sincerity is basic in human character. The sincere man is one in whom is found nothing foreign; he is all of one piece; he has preserved his individuality unviolated.

Sincerity for each man means staying in character with himself. Christ's controversy with the Pharisees centered around their incurable habit of moral play acting. The Pharisee constantly pretended to be what he was not. He attempted to vacate his own "I-ness" and appear in that of another and better man. He assumed a false character and played it for effect. Christ said he was a hypocrite.

It is more than an etymological accident that the word "hypocrite" comes from the stage. It means actor. With that instinct for fitness which usually marks word origins, it has been used to signify one who has violated his sincerity and is playing a false part. An actor is one who assumes a character other than his own and plays it for effect. The more fully he can become possessed by another personality the better he is as an actor.

Bacon has said something to the effect that there are some professions of such nature that the more skillfully a man can work at them the worse man he is. That perfectly describes the profession of acting. Stepping out of our own character for any reason is always dangerous, and may be fatal to the soul. However innocent his intentions, a man who assumes a false character has betrayed his own soul and has deeply injured something sacred within him.

No one who has been in the presence of the Most Holy One, who has felt how high is the solemn privilege of bearing His image, will ever again consent to play a part or to trifle with that most sacred thing, his own deep sincere heart. He will thereafter be constrained to be no one but himself, to preserve reverently the sincerity of his own soul.

In order to produce a religious movie someone must, for the time, disguise his individuality and simulate that of another. His actions must be judged fraudulent, and those who watch them with approval share in the fraud. To pretend to pray, to simulate godly sorrow, to play at worship before the camera for effect—how utterly shocking to the reverent heart! How can Christians who approve this gross pretense ever understand the value of sincerity as taught by our Lord? What will be the end of a generation of Christians fed on such a diet of deception disguised as the faith of our fathers?

A. W. Tozer

The plea that all this must be good because it is done for the glory of God is a gossamer-thin bit of rationalizing which should not fool anyone above the mental age of six. Such an argument parallels the evil rule of expediency which holds the end is everything, and sanctifies the means, however evil, if only the end be commendable. The wise student of history will recognize this immoral doctrine. The Spirit-led Church will have no part of it.

It is not uncommon to find around the theater human flotsam and jetsam washed up by the years, men and women who have played false parts so long that the power to be sincere has forever gone from them. They are doomed to everlasting duplicity. Every act of their lives is faked, every smile is false, every tone of their voice artificial. The curse does not come causeless. It is not by chance that the actor's profession has been notoriously dissolute. Hollywood and Broadway are two sources of corruption which may yet turn America into a Sodom and lay her glory in the dust.

The profession of acting did not originate with the Hebrews. It is not a part of the divine pattern. The Bible mentions it, but never approves it. Drama, as it has come down to us, had its rise in Greece. It was originally a part of the worship of the god Dionysus and was carried on with drunken revelry.

The Miracle Plays of medieval times have been brought forward to justify the modern religious movie. That is an unfortunate weapon to choose for the defense of the movie, for it will surely harm the man who uses it more than any argument I could think of just offhand.

God Still Speaks

The Miracle Plays had their big run in the Middle Ages. They were dramatic performances with religious themes staged for the entertainment of the populace. At their best they were misguided efforts to teach spiritual truths by dramatic representation; at their worst they were shockingly irreverent and thoroughly reprehensible. In some of them the Eternal God was portrayed as an old man dressed in white with a gilt wig! To furnish low comedy, the devil himself was introduced on the stage and allowed to cavort for the amusement of the spectators. Bible themes were used, as in the modern movie, but this did not save the whole thing from becoming so corrupt that the Roman Church had finally to prohibit its priests from having any further part in it.

Those who would appeal for precedent to the Miracle Plays have certainly overlooked some important facts. For instance, the vogue of the Miracle Play coincided exactly with the most dismally corrupt period the Church has ever known. When the Church emerged at last from its long moral night these plays lost popularity and finally passed away. And be it remembered, the instrument God used to bring the Church out of the darkness was not drama; it was the biblical one of Spirit-baptized preaching. Serious-minded men thundered the truth and the people turned to God.

Indeed, history will show that no spiritual advance, no revival, no upsurge of spiritual life has ever been associated with acting in any form. The Holy Spirit never honors pretense.

Can it be that the historic pattern is being repeated? That the appearance of the religious movie is symptomatic of the low state of spiritual health we are in today? I fear so.

A. W. Tozer

Only the absence of the Holy Spirit from the pulpit and lack of true discernment on the part of professing Christians can account for the spread of religious drama among so-called evangelical churches. A Spirit-filled church could not tolerate it.

4. They who present the gospel movie owe it to the public to give biblical authority for their act: and this they have not done.

The Church, as long as it is following the Lord, goes along in Bible ways and can give a scriptural reason for its conduct. Its members meet at stated times to pray together: This has biblical authority back of it. They gather to hear the Word of God expounded: this goes back in almost unbroken continuity to Moses. They sing psalms and hymns and spiritual songs: so they are commanded by the apostle. They visit the sick and relieve the sufferings of the poor: for this they have both precept and example in Holy Writ. They lay up their gifts and bring them at stated times to the church or chapel to be used in the Lord's work: this also follows the scriptural pattern. They teach and train and instruct; they appoint teachers and pastors and missionaries and send them out to do the work for which the Spirit has gifted them: all this has plain scriptural authority behind it. They baptize, then break bread and witness to the lost; they cling together through thick and thin; they bear each other's burdens and share each other's sorrows: this is as it should be, and for all this there is full authority.

Now, for the religious movie where is the authority? For such a serious departure from the ancient pattern, where is the authority? For introducing into the Church the pagan art of acting, where is the authority? Let the movie advocates quote just one verse, from any book of the Bible, in any translation, to justify its use. This they cannot do. The best they can do is to appeal to the world's psychology or repeat brightly that "modern times call for modern methods." But the Scriptures—quote from them one verse to authorize movie acting as an instrument of the Holy Ghost. This they cannot do.

Every sincere Christian must find scriptural authority for the religious movie or reject it, and every producer of such movies, if he would square himself before the faces of honest and reverent men, must either show scriptural credentials or go out of business.

But, says someone, there is nothing unscriptural about the religious movie; it is merely a new medium for the utterance of the old message, as printing is a newer and better method of writing and the radio an amplification of familiar human speech.

To this I reply: The movie is not the modernization or improvement of any scriptural method; rather it is a medium in itself wholly foreign to the Bible and altogether unauthorized therein. It is play acting—just that, and nothing more. It is the introduction into the work of God of that which is not neutral, but entirely bad. The printing press is neutral; so is the radio; so is the camera. They may be used for good or bad purposes at the will of the user. But play acting is bad in its essence in that it involves the simulation of emotions not actually felt. It embodies a gross moral contradiction in that it calls a lie to the service of truth.

Arguments for the religious movie are sometimes clever and always shallow, but there is never any real attempt to cite scriptural authority. Anything that can be said for the movie can be said also for aesthetic dancing, which is a highly touted medium for teaching religious truth by appeal to the eye. Its advocates grow eloquent in its praise—but where is it indicated in the blueprint?

5. God has ordained four methods only by which Truth shall prevail—and the religious movie is not one of them.

Without attempting to arrange these methods in order of importance, they are (1) prayer, (2) song, (3) proclamation of the message by means of words, and (4) good works. These are the four main methods which God has blessed. All other biblical methods are subdivisions of these and stay within their framework.

Notice these in order:

(1) Spirit-burdened prayer. This has been through the centuries a powerful agent for the spread of saving truth among men. A praying Church carried the message of the cross to the whole known world within two centuries after the coming of the Holy Spirit at Pentecost. Read the book of Acts and see what prayer has done and can do when it is made in true faith.

(2) Spirit-inspired song has been another mighty instrument in the spread of the Word among mankind. When the Church sings in the Spirit she draws men unto Christ. Where her song has been ecstatic expression of resurrection joy, it has acted wonderfully to prepare hearts for the saving message. This has no reference to professional religious singers, expensive choirs nor the popular "gospel" chorus. These for the time we leave out of consideration. But I think no one will deny that the sound of a Christian hymn sung by sincere and humble

persons can have a tremendous and permanent effect for good. The Welsh revival is a fair modern example of this.

(3) In the Old Testament, as well as in the New, when God would impart His mind to men He embodied it in a message and sent men out to proclaim it. This was done by means of speaking and writing on the part of the messenger. It was received by hearing and reading on the part of those to whom it was sent. We are all familiar with the verse, "Speak ye comfortably to Jerusalem, and cry unto her" (Isaiah 40:2). John the Baptist was called "The voice of one crying in the wilderness" (Matthew 3:3). Again we have, "And I heard a voice from heaven saying unto me, Write" (Revelation 14:13). And the Apostle John opens his great work called the Revelation by pronouncing a blessing upon him that readeth and them that bear and keep the words of the prophecy and the things which are written therein. The two words "proclaim" and "publish" sum up God's will as it touches His Word. In the Bible, men for the most part wrote what had been spoken; in our time men are commissioned to speak what has been written. In both cases the agent is a word, never a picture, a dance or a pageant.

(4) By His healing deeds our Lord opened the way for His saving Words. He went about doing good, and His Church is commanded to do the same. Faber understood this when he wrote:

"And preach thee too, as love knows how

By kindly deeds and virtuous life."

Church history is replete with instances of missionaries and teachers who prepared the way for their message with deeds of mercy shown to men and women who were at first hostile but who melted under the warm rays of practical kindnesses shown to them in time of need. If anyone should object to calling good works a method, I would not argue the point. Perhaps it would be more accurate to say that they are an overflow into everyday life of the reality of what is being proclaimed.

These are God's appointed methods, set forth in the Bible and confirmed in centuries of practical application. The intrusion of other methods is unscriptural, unwarranted and in violation of spiritual laws as old as the world.

The whole preach-the-gospel-with-movies idea is founded upon the same basic assumptions as modernism—namely, that the Word of God is not final, and that we of this day have a perfect right to add to it or alter it wherever we think we can improve it.

A brazen example of this attitude came to my attention recently. Preliminary printed matter has been sent out announcing that a new organization is in process of being formed. It is to be called the "International Radio and Screen Artists Guild," and one of its two major objectives is to promote the movie as a medium for the spread of the gospel. Its sponsors, apparently, are not Modernists, but confessed Fundamentalists. Some of its declared purposes are: to produce movies "with or without a Christian slant"; to raise and maintain higher standards in the movie field (this would be done, it says here, by having "much prayer" with leaders of the movie industry); to "challenge people, especially young people, to those fields as they are challenged to go to foreign fields."

GOD STILL SPEAKS

This last point should not be allowed to pass without some of us doing a little challenging on our own account. Does this new organization actually propose in seriousness to add another gift to the gifts of the Spirit listed in the New Testament? To the number of the Spirit's gifts, such as pastor, teacher, evangelist, is there now to be added another, the gift of the movie actor? To the appeal for consecrated Christian young people to serve as missionaries on the foreign field is there to be added an appeal for young people to serve as movie actors? That is exactly what this new organization does propose in cold type over the signature of its temporary chairman. Instead of the Holy Spirit saying, "Separate me Barnabas and Saul for the work whereunto I have called them" (Acts 13:2), these people will make use of what they call a "Christian talent listing," to consist of the names of "Christian" actors who have received the Spirit's gift to be used in making religious movies.

Thus the order set up in the New Testament is openly violated, and by professed lovers of the gospel who say unto Jesus, "Lord, Lord," but openly set aside His Lordship whenever they desire. No amount of smooth talk can explain away this serious act of insubordination.

Saul lost a kingdom when he "forced" himself and took profane liberties with the priesthood. Let these movie preachers look to their crown. They may find themselves on the road to En-dor some dark night soon.

6. The religious movie is out of harmony with the whole spirit of the Scriptures and contrary to the mood of true godliness.

A. W. Tozer

To harmonize the spirit of the religious movie with the spirit of the Sacred Scriptures is impossible. Any comparison is grotesque and, if it were not so serious, would be downright funny. To imagine Elijah appearing before Ahab with a roll of film! Imagine Peter standing up at Pentecost and saying, "Let's have the lights out, please." When Jeremiah hesitated to prophesy, on the plea that he was not a fluent speaker, God touched his mouth and said, "I have put my words in thy mouth." Perhaps Jeremiah could have gotten on well enough without the divine touch if he had had a good 16mm projector and a reel of home-talent film.

Let a man dare to compare his religious movie show with the spirit of the Book of Acts. Let him try to find a place for it in the twelfth chapter of First Corinthians. Let him set it beside Savonarola's passionate preaching or Luther's thundering or Wesley's heavenly sermons or Edwards' awful appeals. If he cannot see the difference in kind, then he is too blind to be trusted with leadership in the Church of the Living God. The only thing that he can do appropriate to the circumstances is to drop to his knees and cry with poor Bartimaeus, "Lord, that I might receive my sight."

But some say, "We do not propose to displace the regular method of preaching the gospel. We only want to supplement it." To this I answer: If the movie is needed to supplement anointed preaching it can only be because God's appointed method is inadequate and the movie can do something which God's appointed method cannot do. What is that thing? We freely grant that the movie can produce effects which preaching cannot produce (and which it should never try to produce), but dare we strive for such effects in the light of God's revealed will and in the face of the judgment and a long eternity?

7. I am against the religious movie because of the harmful effect upon everyone associated with it.

First, the evil effect upon the "actors" who play the part of the various characters in the show; this is not the less because it is unsuspected. Who can, while in a state of fellowship with God, dare to play at being a prophet? Who has the gall to pretend to be an apostle, even in a show? Where is his reverence? Where is his fear? Where is his humility? Any one who can bring himself to act a part for any purpose, must first have grieved the Spirit and silenced His voice within the heart. Then the whole business will appear good to him. "He feedeth on ashes; a deceived heart has turned him aside" (Isaiah 44:20). But he cannot escape the secret working of the ancient laws of the soul. Something high and fine and grand will die within him; and worst of all he will never suspect it. That is the curse that follows self-injury always. The Pharisees were examples of this. They were walking dead men, and they never dreamed how dead they were.

Secondly, it identifies religion with the theatrical world. I have seen recently in a fundamentalist magazine an advertisement of a religious film which would be altogether at home on the theatrical page on any city newspaper. Illustrated with the usual sex-bate picture of a young man and young woman in tender embrace, and spangled with such words as "feature-length, drama, pathos, romance," it reeked of Hollywood and the cheap movie house. By such business we are selling out our Christian separation, and nothing but grief can come of it late or soon.

A. W. Tozer

Thirdly, the taste for drama which these pictures develop in the minds of the young will not long remain satisfied with the inferior stuff the religious movie can offer. Our young people will demand the real thing; and what can we reply when they ask why they should not patronize the regular movie house?

Fourthly, the rising generation will naturally come to look upon religion as another, and inferior, form of amusement. In fact, the present generation Yahwist has done this to an alarming extent already, and the gospel movie feeds the notion by fusing religion and fun in the name of orthodoxy. It takes no great insight to see that the religious movie must become increasingly more thrilling as the tastes of the spectators become more and more stimulated.

Fifthly, the religious movie is the lazy preacher's friend. If the present vogue continues to spread it will not be long before any man with enough ability to make an audible prayer, and mentality enough to focus a projector, will be able to pass for a prophet of the Most High God. The man of God can play around all week long and come up to the Lord's Day without a care. Everything has been done for him at the studio. He has only to set up the screen and lower the lights, and the rest follows painlessly.

Wherever the movie is used the prophet is displaced by the projector. The least that such displaced prophets can do is to admit that they are technicians and not preachers. Let them admit that they are not God-sent men, ordained of God for a sacred work. Let them put away their pretense.

God Still Speaks

Allowing that there may be some who have been truly called and gifted of God but who have allowed themselves to be taken in by this new plaything, the danger to such is still great. As long as they can fall back upon the movie, the pressure that makes preachers will be wanting. The habit and rhythm which belong to great preaching will be missing from their ministry. However great their natural gifts, however real their enduement of power, still they will never rise. They cannot while this broken reed lies close at hand to aid them in the crisis. The movie will doom them to be ordinary.

In conclusion

One thing may bother some earnest souls: why so many good people approve the religious movie. The list of those who are enthusiastic about it includes many who cannot be written off as borderline Christians. If it is an evil, why have not these denounced it?

The answer is, lack of spiritual discernment. Many who are turning to the movie are the same who have, by direct teaching or by neglect, discredited the work of the Holy Spirit. They have apologized for the Spirit and so hedged Him in by their unbelief that it has amounted to an out-and-out repudiation. Now we are paying the price for our folly. The light has gone out and good men are forced to stumble around in the darkness of the human intellect.

The religious movie is at present undergoing a period of gestation and seems about to swarm over the churches like a cloud of locusts out of the earth. The figure is accurate; they are coming from below, not from above. The whole modern psychology has been prepared for this invasion of insects. The fundamentalists have become weary of manna and are longing for red flesh. What they are getting is a sorry substitute for the lusty and uninhibited pleasures of the world, but I suppose it is better than nothing, and it saves face by pretending to be spiritual.

Let us not for the sake of peace keep still while men without spiritual insight dictate the diet upon which God's children shall feed. I heard the president of a Christian college say some time ago that the Church is suffering from an "epidemic of amateurism." That remark is sadly true, and the religious movie represents amateurism gone wild. Unity among professing Christians is to be desired, but not at the expense of righteousness. It is good to go with the flock, but I for one refuse mutely to follow a misled flock over a precipice.

If God has given wisdom to see the error of religious shows we owe it to the Church to oppose them openly. We dare not take refuge in "guilty silence." Error is not silent; it is highly vocal and amazingly aggressive. We dare not be less so. But let us take heart: there are still many thousands of Christian people who grieve to see the world take over. If we draw the line and call attention to it we may be surprised how many people will come over on our side and help us drive from the Church this latest invader, the spirit of Hollywood.

THE END

About CrossReach Publications

Thank you for choosing CrossReach Publications.

Trust. Inspiration. Hope.

These three words sum up the philosophy of why CrossReach Publications exist. You want solid Christian books from respected and acknowledged writers from yesteryear, in affordable, quality editions. We want to provide that to you.

Not only do you get the works of the most well-known men and women of Christendom, we have also brought back many lesser-known works from some of the giants from Church history, as well as hidden gems from less popular, and even almost forgotten authors that we believe deserve to be heard again, rather than be lost in the mists of time.

Not only that, our editions are also high quality. We spend time editing and formatting and looking over our manuscripts before publishing. Some small publishers of classic works publish sloppy, almost illegible reproductions of these works. This will not do. We aspire to excellence and we believe it shows in our editions. We cannot guarantee perfection, but we'll try. And we do this at a cost that is right for you.

If you have questions, comments or suggestions about our publications contact us:

ContactUs@CrossReach.net
https://www.CrossReach.store

Don't forget you can follow us on Facebook and Twitter, (addresses are on the copyright page above) to keep up to date on our newest titles and deals.

BESTSELLING TITLES FROM CROSSREACH

How to Be Filled with the Holy Spirit
A. W. Tozer

Before we deal with the question of how to be filled with the Holy Spirit, there are some matters which first have to be settled. As believers you have to get them out of the way, and right here is where the difficulty arises. I have been afraid that my listeners might have gotten the idea somewhere that I had a how-to-be-filled-with-the-Spirit-in-five-easy-lessons doctrine, which I could give you. If you can have any such vague ideas as that, I can only stand before you and say, "I am sorry"; because it isn't true; I can't give you such a course. There are some things, I say, that you have to get out of the way, settled.

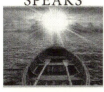

God Still Speaks
A. W. Tozer

Tozer is as popular today as when he was living on the earth. He is respected right across the spectrum of Christianity, in circles that would disagree sharply with him doctrinally. Why is this? A. W. Tozer was a man who knew the voice of God. He shared this experience with every true child of God. With all those who are called by the grace of God to share in the mystical union that is possible with Him through His Son Jesus.

Tozer fought against much dryness and formality in his day. Considered a mighty man of God by most Evangelicals today, he was unconventional in his approach to spirituality and had

---

[2] Buy from CrossReach Publications for quality and price. We have a full selection of titles in print and eBook. All available on the Amazon and Createspace stores. You can see our full selection just by searching for CrossReach Publications in the search bar!

no qualms about consulting everyone from Catholic Saints to German Protestant mystics for inspiration on how to experience God more fully.

Tozer, just like his Master, doesn't fit neatly into our theological boxes. He was a man after God's own heart and was willing to break the rules (man-made ones that is) to get there.

Here are two writings by Tozer that touch on the heart of this goal. Revelation is Not Enough and The Speaking Voice. A bonus chapter The Menace of the Religious Movie is included.

This is meat to sink your spiritual teeth into. Tozer's writings will show you the way to satisfy your spiritual hunger.

The Two Babylons
Alexander Hislop

Fully Illustrated High Res. Images. Complete and Unabridged.

Expanded Seventh Edition. This is the first and only seventh edition available in a modern digital edition. Nothing is left out! New material not found in the first six editions!!! Available in eBook and paperback edition exclusively from CrossReach Publications.

"In his work on "The Two Babylons" Dr. Hislop has proven conclusively that all the idolatrous systems of the nations had their origin in what was founded by that mighty Rebel, the beginning of whose kingdom was Babel (Gen. 10:10)."—A. W. Pink, The Antichrist (1923)

There is this great difference between the works of men and the works of God, that the same minute and searching investigation, which displays the defects and imperfections of the one, brings out also the beauties of the other. If the most finely polished needle on which the art of man has been expended be subjected to a microscope, many inequalities, much roughness and clumsiness, will be seen. But if the microscope be brought to bear on the flowers of the field, no such result appears. Instead of their beauty diminishing, new beauties and still more delicate, that have escaped the naked eye, are forthwith discovered; beauties that make us appreciate, in a way which otherwise we could have had little conception of, the full force of the Lord's saying, "Consider the lilies of the field, how they grow; they toil not, neither do they spin: and yet I say unto you, That even Solomon, in all his glory, was not arrayed like one of these." The same law appears also in comparing the Word of God and the most finished productions of men. There are spots and blemishes in the most admired productions of human genius. But the more the Scriptures are searched, the more minutely they are studied, the more their perfection appears; new beauties are brought into light every day; and the discoveries of science, the researches of the learned, and the labours of infidels, all alike conspire to illustrate the wonderful harmony of all the parts, and the Divine beauty that clothes the whole. If this be the case with Scripture in general, it is especially the case with prophetic Scripture. As every spoke in the wheel of Providence revolves, the prophetic symbols start into still more bold and beautiful relief. This is very strikingly the case with the prophetic language that forms the groundwork and cornerstone of the present work. There never has been any difficulty in the mind of any enlightened Protestant in identifying the woman "sitting on seven mountains," and having on her forehead the name written, "Mystery, Babylon the Great," with the Roman apostacy.

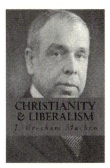

Christianity and Liberalism
J. Gresham Machen

The purpose of this book is not to decide the religious issue of the present day, but merely to present the issue as sharply and clearly as possible, in order that the reader may be aided in deciding it for himself. Presenting an issue sharply is indeed by no means a popular business at the present time; there are many who prefer to fight their intellectual battles in what Dr. Francis L. Patton has aptly called a "condition of low visibility." Clear-cut definition of terms in religious matters, bold facing of the logical implications of religious views, is by many persons regarded as an impious proceeding. May it not discourage contribution to mission boards? May it not hinder the progress of consolidation, and produce a poor showing in columns of Church statistics? But with such persons we cannot possibly bring ourselves to agree. Light may seem at times to be an impertinent intruder, but it is always beneficial in the end. The type of religion which rejoices in the pious sound of traditional phrases, regardless of their meanings, or shrinks from "controversial" matters, will never stand amid the shocks of life. In the sphere of religion, as in other spheres, the things about which men are agreed are apt to be the things that are least worth holding; the really important things are the things about which men will fight.

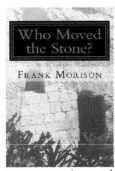

Who Moved the Stone?
Frank Morison

This study is in some ways so unusual and provocative that the writer thinks it desirable to state here very briefly how the book came to take its present form. In one sense it could have taken no other, for it is essentially a confession, the inner story of a man who originally set out to write one kind of book and found himself compelled by the sheer force of circumstances to write another.

It is not that the facts themselves altered, for they are recorded imperishably in the monuments and in the pages of human history. But the interpretation to be put upon the facts underwent a change. Somehow the perspective shifted—not suddenly, as in a flash of insight or inspiration, but slowly, almost imperceptibly, by the very stubbornness of the facts themselves.

The book as it was originally planned was left high and dry, like those Thames barges when the great river goes out to meet the incoming sea. The writer discovered one day that not only could he no longer write the book as he had once conceived it, but that he would not if he could.

To tell the story of that change, and to give the reasons for it, is the main purpose of the following pages.

What We Are In Christ
E. W. Kenyon

I was surprised to find that the expressions "in Christ," "in whom," and "in Him" occur more than 130 times in the New Testament. This is the heart of the Revelation of Redemption given to Paul. Here is the secret of faith—faith that conquers, faith that moves mountains. Here is the secret of the Spirit's guiding us into all reality. The heart craves intimacy with the Lord Jesus and with the Father. This craving can now be satisfied.

Ephesians 1:7: "In whom we have our redemption through his blood, the remission of our trespasses according to the riches of his grace."

It is not a beggarly Redemption, but a real liberty in Christ that we have now. It is a Redemption by the God Who could say, "Let there be lights in the firmament of heaven," and cause the whole starry heavens to leap into being in a single instant. It is Omnipotence beyond human reason. This is where philosophy has never left a footprint.

Claiming Our Rights
E. W. Kenyon

There is no excuse for the spiritual weakness and poverty of the Family of God when the wealth of Grace and Love of our great Father with His power and wisdom are all at our disposal. We are not coming to the Father as a tramp coming to the door begging for food; we come as sons not only claiming our legal rights but claiming the natural rights of a child that is begotten in love. No one can hinder us or question our right of approach to our Father.

Satan has Legal Rights over the sinner that God cannot dispute or challenge. He can sell them as slaves; he owns them, body, soul and spirit. But the moment we are born again... receive Eternal Life, the nature of God,—his legal dominion ends.

Christ is the Legal Head of the New Creation, or Family of God, and all the Authority that was given Him, He has given us: (Matthew 28:18), "All authority in heaven," the seat of authority, and "on earth," the place of execution of authority. He is "head over all things," the highest authority in the Universe, for the benefit of the Church which is His body.

Elementary Geography
Charlotte Mason

This little book is confined to very simple "reading lessons upon the Form and Motions of the Earth, the Points of the Compass, the Meaning of a Map: Definitions."

It is hoped that these reading lessons may afford intelligent teaching, even in the hands of a young teacher.

Children should go through the book twice, and should, after the second reading, be able to answer any of the questions from memory.

The Person and Work of the Holy Spirit
R. A. Torey

Before one can correctly understand the work of the Holy Spirit, he must first of all know the Spirit Himself. A frequent source of error and fanaticism about the work of the Holy Spirit is the attempt to study and understand His work without first of all coming to know Him as a Person.

It is of the highest importance from the standpoint of worship that we decide whether the Holy Spirit is a Divine Person, worthy to receive our adoration, our faith, our love, and our entire surrender to Himself, or whether it is simply an influence emanating from God or a power or an illumination that God imparts to us. If the Holy Spirit is a person, and a Divine Person, and we do not know Him as such, then we are robbing a Divine Being of the worship and the faith and the love and the surrender to Himself which are His due.

In His Steps
Charles M. Sheldon

The sermon story, In His Steps, or "What Would Jesus Do?" was first written in the winter of 1896, and read by the author, a chapter at a time, to his Sunday evening congregation in the Central Congregational Church, Topeka, Kansas. It was then printed as a serial in The Advance (Chicago), and its reception by the readers of that paper was such that the publishers of The Advance made arrangements for its appearance in book form. It was their desire, in which the author heartily joined, that the story might reach as many readers as possible, hence succeeding editions of paper-covered volumes at a price within the reach of nearly all readers.

The story has been warmly and thoughtfully welcomed by Endeavor societies, temperance organizations, and Y. M. C. A. 's. It is the earnest prayer of the author that the book may go its way with a great blessing to the churches for the quickening of Christian discipleship, and the hastening of the Master's kingdom on earth.

WE OFFER A LARGE & GROWING SELECTION OF CHRISTIAN TITLES
ALL AVAILABLE ON THE AMAZON & CREATESPACE STORES
JUST SEARCH FOR CROSSREACH PUBLICATIONS!

Made in the USA
Monee, IL
06 March 2020